Poles Apart

Challenges for Business

in the Digital Age

Kate Baucherel

Paperback ISBN

Published in the UK by MX Publishing

335 Princess Park Manor, Royal Drive, London, N11 3GX

www.mxpublishing.co.uk (UK & Europe)

www.mxpublishing.com (USA)

Cover design and illustrations by Jordan McCord
Cover photography © Martin Ker Photography

Poles Apart:
Challenges for Business in the Digital Age

The internet gives us access to the whole world to build business. But many SMEs are Poles Apart: sitting in the cold, and missing out on the huge potential that the online space can offer.

This is as true for the smallest businesses in the country as it is for large established organisations, where employees themselves are Poles Apart and the clash of cultures is causing turbulence. As processes and procedures become outdated and the world moves on around them, businesses fight internally to balance risks and rewards.

Getting a business properly connected is simple, but can be a daunting prospect for people with less fluent digital skills. Doing business online also opens up a Pandora's Box of potential pitfalls as communication methods change and the lines between personal and business connections blur.

There are huge benefits to having your business online – but the risks you recognise depend on your point of view. Are you excited by the internet and the potential it offers, but not fully aware of the risks? You have the world at your feet, Polar Bear, but a journey to make. Or are you all too aware of the commercial minefield, and wary of diving in? It's time for Penguins to take the plunge.

So, are you a Penguin or a Polar Bear? What skills do you need, and what risks do you face, to make the journey to warmer climes?

The Digital Challenge

The pace of technological change over the past 20 years has created a divide in business. Largely age-related, there is a yawning gulf between the online mindsets of young employees and entrepreneurs, and traditional approach of more mature employers and business startups.

Who is this book for?

Anyone who is in business – whether you are working on your own or as part of a larger organisation – needs to be aware of the risks and rewards of engaging in the online space, and how to reconcile the different viewpoints across this digital skills spectrum.

For new small businesses at both ends of the scale, there are risks which can affect the success of the enterprise. We see people either doing too much without understanding the commercial implications – the Polar Bear approach, or doing too little out of caution and misplaced prudence – Penguins.

There's danger for the old guard and large organisations, too. The entrepreneurs of the 1980s, historic family firms, and public bodies had already established their businesses, markets and processes before the World Wide Web exploded into our lives in 1993. Not only do these organisations need to stay in touch with their long-established customer base, but they also have a challenge both for internal security and business processes and procedures as young tech-savvy recruits come into direct contact and conflict with a senior management steeped in more traditional business practices.

Business is better when you're connected

A report commissioned by Go On UK – the charity dedicated to making the UK the world's most digitally skilled nation - and published by Booz & Company in 2012 showed that "only one third of small and medium-sized companies in the UK have a digital presence and only 14% sell their products and services online, missing out on the potential for billions of pounds more revenue".

Why are only 1 in 7 UK SMEs selling their products and services online? What are the barriers that are preventing the rest from making the leap? If you are holding back, this book can help you understand why, and prepare you to discover a new world!

What about the 2/3 of businesses without a digital presence which they control? Of course, most businesses are somewhere online without knowing it – and the information's usually wrong (see the chapter on Understanding your Digital Footprint below). Just having a tiny foothold online, a place where your customers can see you as they surf, can make a difference to your credibility and how easily people find you.

The turnover of small businesses could be boosted by as much as £18.8 billion if all SMEs sold and marketed online.

Would you like a slice of this amazing online potential?

Figures from the Office of National Statistics, published in 2013, make a strong case. 67% of UK adults now go online to research and purchase goods and services. If only one third of enterprises are active online, does that mean they're getting twice the business? The maths isn't that easy, but there's certainly a widening gap between the connected and the rest.

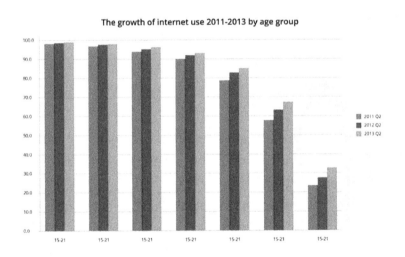

The growth of internet use 2011-2013 by age group

Increasingly, people will expect to find you online. Are you as visible as your competitors? Are you dealing with your customers through social media, email and other channels? Are you safe in the digital world?

Over the past two years, the numbers online have grown in all age groups, most noticeably the over 55s, 65s and 75s. Spending decisions, if not the purchases themselves, are being made online by the majority of the population. If you think that your market demographic is too old to be influenced by how you appear online, then think again!

You need to be online because the web is where your customers are.

Still not convinced? You may find yourself out in the cold.

Discover a new world

To grasp all this potential, and simultaneously manage the risks of working online, you need to know where you (and your colleagues) are starting from.

So, are you a Penguin, looking up at the rich pickings but without the online experience to take them, or a Polar Bear, with the world at your feet – but a lot to learn on the way?

This book will help you to:

- Decide if you are a Penguin or a Polar Bear, and why.

- Establish common ground between the two extremes.

- Understand the risks and rewards of doing business online.

- Keep your business safe, and on the right side of the law.

- Take simple steps to getting it right on the internet.

- Manage and build your Digital Footprint for online visibility.

- Improve communication and the customer service you deliver.

- Take responsibility for your organisation's online development.

- Build your digital skills!

Penguin or Polar Bear?

Let's look at the two extremes of online engagement. These are generalisations, very two-dimensional sketches, but it's likely that most people will recognise to which camp they (or their colleagues) belong, to a greater or lesser extent.

The goal is to balance the strengths of each extreme, minimise all the risks of doing business online, and come in from the cold to the profitable equatorial warmth.

Polar Bears
Young entrepreneurs communicate online as second nature –

they've probably used computers since nursery school - but often fail to recognise dangers and legal pitfalls which more experienced business people avoid. Polar Bears think their whole market is online, but may have missed an untapped offline element with cash to spend, and with it an opportunity to build both their business and the economy.

There's a tendency for Polar Bears to rush in without understanding the wider implications of their actions, and to get frustrated with people who are not as fast to adopt new technologies.

Having digital skills at their fingertips does not mean they are immediately able or willing to help others to develop those skills: teaching and helping, disseminating knowledge, is a skill in itself.

Polar Bears will have an important role to play as their experience widens and their ability to cascade their skills through an organisation, or train and help their clients, improves.

Penguins

Anyone over the age of 45 – leaving school in the mid-1980s - will not have used computers as a matter of course at school. Generally this age group continues to be a late adopter, even if they are using business tools (spreadsheets, word processing and management systems) on a daily basis.

For a Penguin, there's competition coming from more tech-savvy newcomers who can access markets online without thinking about it – and danger coming from young employees and colleagues who may not recognise the divide between business and personal communication, or the risks involved when those lines blur.

Penguins are caught between the devil and the deep blue sea. If they avoid the online space because they don't understand it, there's a lost opportunity and potentially considerable damage which can be done to their business without their knowledge. If they delegate action ("we need to get online – can you do it?") there is an equally grave risk that the business is either wrongly represented online, or more seriously that it runs legal risks either in publishing the wrong information or mismanaging the new communication channels in the organisation.

Equatorial Warmth

Half way through a full career, someone in the 35-44 age group will have accumulated significant corporate experience and an appreciation of the classic risks to a business.

This age group is also at the very tip of the scale of regular online social engagement – for clear historical reasons. In 1982 we saw the advent of BBC computers in schools, and games consoles, word processors and the ZX-81 and ZX-Spectrum arriving in many homes. In 1993 the internet truly opened for business, with CompuServe in the ascendance and emails starting to make headway as a communication tool.

For those people who have followed the trends and stayed abreast of technological developments while simultaneously building their commercial understanding, this is a unique and sought-after position.

There's still a learning curve here, and it's no time to be complacent. If anything, we've learned how fast the world changes and we are open to new things. Tech-savvy as I am, my primary school age children can still surprise me with their mastery of the gadgets they access, and I'm almost running to keep up and control what they do!

Arriving at the mid-point between the two extremes – regardless of age - should be the goal for everyone: taking advantage of new opportunities with your eyes wide open. This is the place where cultures collide, where risks are minimised, and the opportunities are there for the taking.

However, getting to that ideal position at the centre means a journey, and you have to know where you are starting.

So, are you a Penguin or a Polar Bear? Perhaps the SE/CE Curve can help you to decide.

So what is the SE/CE Curve?

Online opportunities and threats differ according to your balance of Social Engagement and Corporate Experience.

A Strongly Social person with limited corporate experience faces the risk that, with easy and informal communication being the norm, there could be an inadvertent transmission of confidential information to third parties, and a lack of separation between work and personal life. There are some great native skills to be harnessed, but increased risks from lack of life experience. These are our Polar Bears.

A Strongly Corporate person with limited online engagement runs the risk that their communication methods don't keep up with the customer base and their target markets, and that failing to move with the times will leave their business in the doldrums. A classic Penguin wants to dive in but sees too many risks ahead.

The SE/CE Curve

The area between the curves represents risks to the business.

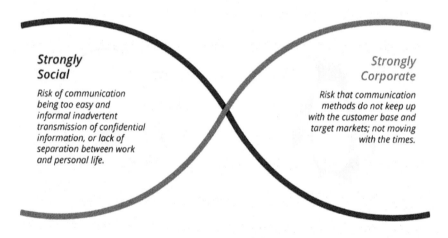

Strongly Social

Risk of communication being too easy and informal inadvertent transmission of confidential information, or lack of separation between work and personal life.

Strongly Corporate

Risk that communication methods do not keep up with the customer base and target markets; not moving with the times.

Social Engagement vs Corporate Experience: The SE/CE Curve

Where do you sit on the SE/CE curve?

Strong Social Engagement – Young Polar Bears

Strong Corporate Experience – Older Penguins

The Future of the SE/CE curve

The SE/CE curve was developed to explain the vastly different attitudes to online business that we encounter in our day to day work with businesses of all sizes and in a huge range of industries. The common factors stood out: embracing the online space but running risks, versus extreme caution holding back the development of a business. Understanding where a client is coming from is half the battle in delivering a strong and workable strategy for them to get connected and build their business online.

Where do you sit on the SE/CE curve?

Your position will help you decide what risks to address and what skills you need to learn in order to build your business safely online.

The two extremes are Strong Social Engagement - the young Polar Bears; and Strong Corporate Experience – the older Penguins. Most people will fall somewhere between the two, but a team of people will represent the whole spectrum.

There's generally a clear age-related profile, simply because of the historical timing of the development of this technology which society now takes for granted. Of course, some older people may be very socially engaged because of the nature of their work, or due to early engagement with technology companies who were using intranets before the internet, and led the movement onto the World Wide Web. There are also younger people at the opposite extreme who may have had a difficult start and have not the opportunity to develop or the need to update their skills, and are in danger of being left behind by rapid change.

This graph published by Digital Trends in April 2013 shows very clearly the skew in the US population, with high online social engagement among the youngest in the workforce, tailing off as people reach their forties.

Population vs. Age

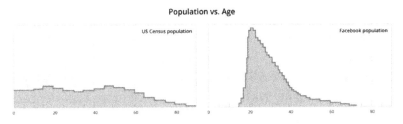

If you don't think that the age profile fits exactly, then reflect on how you use the internet and on your level of confidence and experience in business. This will help to establish where you are starting from, the opportunities you may be missing, and the risk factors you could face on your journey.

Strong Social Engagement – Young Polar Bears

The 16-24 age group represents those people joining the workforce for the first time. Most will be employees, and some may take an early step towards entrepreneurship. This group will have had access to computers and increasingly complex technology from birth. Their level of social engagement is very high: they rely on the online space for communicating, researching, purchasing, and entertainment. It is as natural to this age group to use electronic communication as it was for generations before to pick up the phone or write a postcard.

The risks to a business either employing or being run by this age group are significant. Without the caution of more experienced business people, there are dangers at every turn.

Effectively, informal communication without comprehension of business protocols, and the lack of physical separation between business and personal communication, can result in (among others):

- Inadvertent breach or formation of contracts.

- Contravention of the Data Protection Act.

- Crossing the boundaries of the Equality Act 2010, including harassment.

The biggest legal risks are commercial and employment related, and are covered in more detail in Trials and Tribulations: Legal Risks Online, below.

The people in the 25-34 year old band have a similarly high level of social engagement and more corporate nous, but there will still be some learning to do – and opportunities to teach. As these employees rise through the ranks of large organisations they will start to influence policies and procedures, but will more than likely come into conflict with colleagues and managers who still need to be convinced about the rewards of getting connected.

General risks for the average Polar Bear are less obvious but easier to manage – they involve making sure that the information you put out about your business covers all the legal bases.

- Simple requirements such as those of the Companies Act 2006 to include company registration information on letterhead also apply to any online communications.
- The Data Protection Act 1998, The Companies (Trading Disclosures) Regulations 2008, The Privacy and Electronic Communications (EC Directive) Regulations 2003 and The Electronic Commerce (EC Directive) Regulations 2002 all have something to say about legal requirements for websites including statements of how data is collected and used (Privacy Policies).

These are covered in more detail in Keeping your Website Legal, below.

Strong Corporate Experience – Older Penguins

At the other end of the scale we find established, experienced owners and managers. They know their markets, their strategies, and are almost certainly well versed in the legal pitfalls of traditional business, either through training or bitter experience. They have been in business long enough to be conscious of all the potential risks and pitfalls – 'loose lips sink ships' – but may not realise that the opportunities of getting connected and doing business online are worth the effort.

They will have grown up without the technologies younger staff take for granted, are unlikely to have engaged with computers at work before the late 1980s, and even if they were early adopters of email and intranets, the internet as we know it did not open up until 1993. Most of these senior executives will not be engaging online with social media – although their families and their staff may well be.

The biggest risk for the Penguin is...... DOING NOTHING AT ALL. With the majority of the population in every working age group engaging online (Office for National Statistics 2013), there's a danger of being left behind.

Think of a retail business in a coastal town. With all other factors staying the same, that business will not turn over as much as an identical retailer in an inland town. Why? Because if you draw a circle radiating from the shop, *half of the geographical market is in the sea*.

Now look at your business. Are your competitors selling to a market you can't access? Are half your potential customers out of reach, because you don't have the skills to connect with them? In that case, it's time to dive in!

As with all diving, though, you need to be sure that you can survive in the new environment. Building your own digital skills is essential. Relying on third parties to provide online services without having those basic skills, or any understanding the digital landscape, can waste money and time. Businesses are bombarded daily with offers for online services, many very dubious, others above-board. Unless you have some understanding at the strategic level it's easy to invest in the wrong tools.

The Future of the SE/CE curve

The intersection of Social Engagement and Corporate Experience can at a generalised level be associated with a specific age group. At the moment, this is around the mid-forties – but as it attaches to that group, in 20 years the SE/CE curve will look quite different!

As time goes on, the Social Engagement curve will change markedly - and without doubt, there will be a new factor we can't foresee coming in to play, delivering the same dilemmas to business as those which have existed since the arrival of the telephone over a century ago.

Risks and Rewards

Polar Bears: Potential Leaders with a Steep Learning Curve

Penguins: Overcoming Caution to grab Opportunities

Risks and Rewards for All Online Businesses

Every business is continually reviewing its strengths, weaknesses, opportunities and threats. So let's have a look at the online space from the perspective of each of the Poles.

Polar Bears: Potential Leaders with a Steep Learning Curve

 A Polar Bear – someone with strong social engagement – can communicate fluently online. They have a major **strength** in that they are not afraid to grasp the latest technologies and run with them.

Their greatest **weakness** is the assumption that everyone is equally tech-savvy - and that other people using the online space are doing so for honest purposes.

Polar Bears have a real **opportunity** to build business and the economy if they can help others to improve their digital skills. Their greatest **threats** come from the legal risks and corporate pitfalls which are amplified by the online space. Just because you know how to build a website doesn't mean you know the legalities behind displaying company information. Just because you believe you are responsible online doesn't mean your staff know how to keep their personal and business lives separate. Manage the risks – and deliver an even better service to clients.

This group will not only be the leaders of the future economy, but have the chance to be Digital Champions and help others get connected. By learning to recognise where someone is struggling with a lack of skills, Polar Bears can empathise rather than criticise, and deliver the right training and support to allow their customers and stakeholders to benefit from online opportunities.

A classic example of this is the company whose customers are struggling with using a new website. Instead of getting frustrated, talk to them and see where the skills gap lies. The solution may be as simple as helping someone upgrade from an outdated browser.

Penguins: Overcoming Caution to grab Opportunities

The **strength** of the Penguin – someone with strong corporate experience – is in that very experience: understanding how business and the world works.

Penguins are generally clear about potential problems, but this often makes them risk-averse. This is a real **threat**, as avoiding the online space to minimise issues won't make them go away – and may lead to disaster.

Avoiding a knee-jerk reaction, making the jump online without understanding what is out there, is as much of a threat as inaction. There are hundreds of offers coming out every day from organisations that are less than scrupulous about whom they sell to. If it seems too good to be true, it probably is (first page on Google is a good example, as are extremely cheap websites!). If there seems to be one solution for everyone, it's unlikely to work as well as carefully tailoring the approach. Caveat emptor: buyer beware!

Even relying on a third party can be dangerous. For instance, if a Penguin subcontracts the development of their online presence to a young Polar Bear, whether an employee or a consultant, then they should recognise that there could be some details in this development which are inadvertently overlooked, purely due to a lack of life experience. Making the effort to understand the online business environment (if not the technical background) means that a real working partnership can develop to deliver the best results.

There is no way to prevent information about a business proliferating online. A Digital Footprint can be created without your knowledge, as data in the public domain is bundled and sold and re-used by myriads of agencies. We look at this in more detail later in the chapter on The Communication Revolution.

The clash between Penguins and their tech-savvy colleagues is something that causes a lot of turbulence in larger businesses, too. Where young Polar Bears are keen to push ahead with the latest technology, the Penguin holds back for the most sensible of reasons (security), but without appreciating the opportunity that could be lost without action.

A Penguin's **weakness** in digital skills can be easily addressed by establishing a reason to get online – and recognising the **opportunities** that are out there should be more than enough encouragement! This is the key to making the transition to balanced equatorial warmth.

Risks and Rewards for All Online Businesses

The reward for business is clear: let's recap:

The turnover of small businesses could be boosted by as much as £18.8 billion if all SMEs sold and marketed online.

That alone would be enough to bring most SMEs to the table. But what about the operational benefits of getting connected? Would you like better communication, better information, easier transactions, lower carbon footprints, lower costs? It all adds up to a real business jackpot. We'll look at the best way to exploit the Communication Revolution in more detail later, including using social media effectively and developing customer service and business routines.

The key risks are simple to define, too.

Whether you are a Penguin or a Polar Bear, understanding the legal aspect of online business is vital.

Legal pitfalls, whether in commercial or employment law, and the problems of general business confidentiality and data security, have so many more connotations when you throw online communication into the mix.

Let's look in more detail at the most common risks and rewards. We'll address the legal risks (all the legislation quoted is current as at January 2014), cover the basics of website legalities, think about online security and safety, and how the Communication Revolution has changed the face of business for the better.

Finally, we'll look at what YOU can do to develop your digital skills and business understanding, and take up the challenges of the Digital Age.

Are you ready to do business effectively online?

Trials and Tribulations: Legal Risks Online

The Commercial Basics

Active Communication Risks

    Managing your Human Resources

    Keeping a lid on Pandora's Box

Company Culture Matters

    Perceived risks are not always the right ones

    Bring Your Own Device

Cover the Bases

Potentially the most serious risk for any business is communicating the wrong things over the wrong medium. Lengthy court actions can be won or lost over communication error.

With social media opening communication up across the online space, and the lines between personal and business interactions being increasingly blurred, companies need to take real care.

The Commercial Basics

Our Penguins - business people with strong Corporate Experience - will normally have a good idea of the legal hoops to be jumped through by a company, although they may not realise how much traditional legislation applies to the online space.

Many Polar Bears have no grasp of the legals, either. A classic

problem occurs where a young developer builds a website for a friend: there is often no thought given to the basic legal requirements of the content, or to the risks that might come from communication through that site.

In my business, I spend a lot of time working with clients whose websites have been created by well-meaning and skilled young developers who didn't have the knowledge or experience to realise that there is special content required – but the client didn't know either. The legal requirements fall down a gap between the two. Is it the responsibility of the web designer to get the legals right, or the business owner? Best if both are aware of the issues.

The list is long!

The obvious starting point for a limited company or partnership is the Companies Act 2006 - but UK businesses, whether limited companies, partnerships or sole traders, need to take account of a lot more than this. The Data Protection Act 1998, The Companies (Trading Disclosures) Regulations 2008, The Privacy and Electronic Communications (EC Directive) Regulations 2003 and The Electronic Commerce (EC Directive) Regulations 2002 all have something to say about legal requirements for websites including statements of how data is collected and used (Privacy Policies).

The current requirements of the Companies Act 2006 and other relevant pieces of legislation are covered in the chapter "Keeping your Website Legal" below. Take a look and check that your business is publishing all the right information in emails and on websites. It's a very simple thing to get right – and one less thing to worry about when you do.

Active Communication Risks

The biggest legal stumbling block for business is active communication. There are a range of potential risks that come hand in hand with the trend towards informal communication on email and social media. These include

- Employment matters such as harassment, discrimination and defamation.
- Contractual issues such as accidental formation or breach of contracts.
- Data protection and copyright considerations, including trade secrets being inadvertently revealed.
- IT security including hacking and virus

Managing your Human Resources

Employers may be surprised that harassment, discrimination and defamation come to the top of the list here. Symptomatic of the blurring between business and personal communication, the potential for intended or unintended slights, bullying, and unwanted attention is huge - and if this happens within a group of work colleagues, it's the employer's responsibility to be on top of it; an employer is automatically responsible for the behaviour of employees.

- Circulating an offensive meme? If a colleague takes offence, they have recourse to the Equality Act 2010.

- Someone under stress because they feel they are being harassed, excluded or bullied online? The employer has a responsibility to safeguard their mental health.
- An employee leaves because they object to the behaviour of their colleagues on social media? Constructive dismissal is a possibility.

Ignoring social media, thinking it is a 'personal' matter, can open up a business to costly tribunal claims. For want of a nail the battle was lost: for want of a social media policy, a company can be lost.

Keeping a lid on Pandora's Box

 How does an employer react? How do you keep a lid on Pandora's Box? It's a real minefield, but one which can be navigated with care.

Foremost in your armoury is training: make sure your socially engaged Polar Bears get a taste of the risks that the experienced Penguins take for granted. Educate, train, and guide.

Don't over-react to mistakes or give in to fear! Achieving that strong social engagement is essential to a modern business, and clamping down can be counterproductive. An inappropriate embargo or censoring not only exposes you to commercial risk by failing to reach new markets, but potentially monitoring activity too closely can violate the human rights of your employees!

Work out how communication strategies are going to fit into the day to day routines of your business. Make sure you understand the positive points in social media and email communication, and build a workable strategy, but set the right limits for your organisation and document them properly in the company handbook. Social media is such an important element of business communication these days, but the lines between business and personal communication can be blurred. It's up to the experienced Penguins to decide what is communicated (and what is not) while the tech-savvy Polar Bears use their skills to manage that communication.

The company's culture needs to take account of the new landscape – we are dealing with a paradigm shift, like he generations before us who had to cope with the advent of printing, telegraph and telephone. Knowing where the risks lie and managing them in an open and proactive way reduces your exposure.

Company Culture Matters

When I started work, I learned exactly how to lay out a letter, and how to behave on the telephone, so whatever I said or did represented the business properly. There was a payphone for staff to use for personal calls, and there were no mobiles, so no difficulty drawing the line between personal and business calls. The company's cultural expectation was clear, engrained and

 enforced - and it was easy to control. Of course as a young, impetuous Polar Bear I made mistakes, I was frustrated by the people above me who seemed not to understand the speed of modern life, but I learned the ropes because the culture was strong and policies were carefully enforced.

Perceived risks are not always the right ones

As soon as mobile telephones and office PCs with internet access came into the equation, changes had to be made to handle the novelty of these new means of communication.

Mobile phone use was strictly controlled – although as the phones themselves were the size of bricks and had to recharge for 24 hours this wasn't a tough call. Bills were checked line by line for traces of 'personal calls'. The driver behind control was not the active communication risks, but the cost.

However, emails and intranet didn't come in for the same scrutiny because they were free! The main risk that the company perceived was a financial one – because up until then every method of communication incurred a cost. We eventually learned the hard way about some of the risks discussed above (the offensive meme that hit the office was a real watershed) and as the internet developed it became a fantastic tool for us as a business working all across Europe, and put us ahead of the competition.

Bring Your Own Device

Now, with smartphones and the rise of Bring Your Own Device, the employee controls the means of communication, and there is a whole generation who have grown up without understanding that there are different rules for work and play. The trouble is that getting it wrong at work can have far-reaching implications.

The Information Commissioner's Office – the source of the Data Protection Act – has just issued new guidelines on policies to manage Bring Your Own Device schemes and protect company data. For example, an employee of a large company took photos of documents for new starters (seems sensible, if there's no photocopier) but the smartphone was stolen with the photographs still on – an inadvertent breach of data protection.

Cover the Bases

The workplace is governed by a raft of legislation which protects staff while at work - from each other and from their employer. Particular minefields include harassment, discrimination, defamation, breach of confidentiality, accidental formation or breaching of contracts, data protection breaches, copyright infringement, and hacking or viruses entering the network.

These could all happen in the old days - but the ease and informality of email and social media pose a much bigger risk. Employers may try to control the staff by tight monitoring - but this has its pitfalls: at what point is Big Brother watching you?

To cover all the bases, ensure that what you want is detailed in your company policies, and you engrain those policies into your corporate culture, so that your business can reap the benefits of the internet, not the whirlwind.

Keeping your Website Legal

The Basics

Cookies

Privacy Policy

Payment Data Security

Terms and Conditions

Protecting your own privacy

Anyone in business - as a limited company, a partnership or a sole trader – finds out pretty fast that the law requires certain details on your letterhead, invoices and brochures. But what about the online space? Now that it's so easy to set up a simple template website with a few clicks of a mouse, how many businesses are breaking the law without realising it?

Here's a handy checklist of what you need to have on your website and online communications under UK law, who says you have to, and why it matters.

The Basics

Let's start with the Companies Act 2006, The Companies (Trading Disclosures) Regulations 2008 and The Electronic Commerce (EC Directive) Regulations 2002: Here's what they say, in simple terms:

- Include an actual geographic trading address – no PO Box numbers! This is very important for local search engine results as well.

- Limited Companies and Partnerships need to quote their registered address, their registration number, and (if a partnership) the names of the partners.

- Your contact details including an email address or a contact form which allows people to contact you 'rapidly and in a direct and effective manner'.

- If you are part of a trade register, you need to quote your registration number and details of which register you are in. This is in any case sensible marketing to build trust with prospective customers.

- Your VAT registration number – don't forget the GB prefix.

Once you have these basics – and remember these should be on any emails you send as well as on your website - there are other pieces of legislation to consider.

Cookies

A cookie is a small, usually temporary file that is downloaded to a user's machine when they access most websites. This is normally linked to anonymous data capture software which sits behind most sites for analytics or signup purposes; cookies can also speed up browsing as they keep a snapshot – a cache – of the web page you visited.

Ever typed in the start of a website you visit and have a dropdown list appear? That's them at work. Cookies do not damage the computer and users can, if they know how, set their browser to notify them when they receive a cookie which enables them to decide if they want to accept it or not.

The Privacy and Electronic Communications (EC Directive) Regulations 2003 – the 'Cookie Law' – requires an 'opt-out' button for Cookies. You will see these popping up on websites when you visit them for the first time, telling you that the site uses Cookies and asking if you are happy for data to be collected. This is something of a sledgehammer to crack a nut, as the law was intended to ensure that people knew when the information they typed into a site was being stored up for other purposes, but it applies to the collection of anonymous tracking data and useful temporary files, too.

If you click on the link on a cookie popup, you will be taken to the site's Privacy Policy.

Privacy Policy

If you have a contact form on your site (as opposed to just an email address where people can contact you), or any type of analytics or tracking software, you are capturing data. The Cookie Pop-up, above, keeps you straight with the Privacy and Electronic Communications (EC Directive) Regulations 2003, but to comply with the Data Protection Act 1998 you need to state in your site's Privacy Policy how you will use that data.

This isn't a daunting prospect – if you write down in plain English your exact intentions for the data you collect, then you are within the law. For example, if you have a newsletter signup or a contact form, think about exactly what you do. Do you use that information internally for marketing purposes? Do you pass it to third parties, and if so who and why? As long as you state your intentions, you are complying with the law.

If your business needs to be registered with the Information Controller – mainly professional services such as accountants, HR and so on who hold detailed personal and business data - you also need to quote your registration number in this policy.

Payment Data Security

As soon as you take any payment card details yourself from a customer – over the telephone or online – you need to comply with the "Payment Card Industry Data Security Standards" - PCI DSS regulations. These are very thorough and can be quite daunting.

If you are selling online we recommend starting out with a third-party system to avoid handling card information (e.g. PayPal and others).

You'll need to have a procedure in place for any instance where you take a customer's payment card details. If they are entering their details on a third party system that's fine, as you never touch their card, but as soon as you start taking orders over the phone, for instance, then there are hoops to jump through.

Work with your bank to get the paperwork right and check with your web designer that your ecommerce system is using PCI DSS validated payment software.

Terms and Conditions

Although not legally required, you can save yourself a lot of potential problems by including terms and conditions on your website. We recommend two sets:

One, Terms and Conditions of Website Use, can be used to give all of the details about your business as required by law, such as your registered address (a handy tip for homeworkers who want to keep that information off the face of the website). It should also and to point out to users how far your liability extends for things you say on your site or for access to the site– by that we mean making sure no-one can come back and claim they have suffered a loss because of, for instance, losing their internet connection while on your site. Sounds daft, but this appears in most terms and conditions we've seen!

The other set, Terms and Conditions of Sale, is vital for ecommerce sites – make sure that your customers have the chance to read your terms and conditions of sale before they actually make a purchase, or they will not be legally binding for that sale.

Protecting your own privacy

Home-based traders are sometimes nervous of 'personal' information getting out onto the World Wide Web. However, once you set up in business you will find a lot of your information is available freely through Companies House, HMRC and online directories - and as your "Digital Footprint" grows, you could end up finding before you know it that Google's automatically generated Local Page is showing a picture of your house!

There's more detail about the way a Digital Footprint is created, and how you can control it, in the chapter on The Communication Revolution, below. Be aware always that what is out there on the internet was not necessarily put there by you. You don't know where your information ends up in the digital age. However, as long as everything that you put online is correct, and you know where to go to keep those details up to date, you have a good degree of control.

Connected and Protected: Staying Safe Online

Getting your Social Media right

Protecting your online presence

Penguins: Aware of the danger, but can still be caught out online.

Polar Bears: Susceptible to temptation, without understanding the risks.

Perfect Password Practice

Data security within your business

Securing your website

The Ticking Browser Timebomb

Why is there a problem?

A small step to make a difference

In the vast majority of UK SMEs, responsibility for business communication falls to one person at the top of the organisation. But what happens as the business grows?

It's time to think about how social media and email communication is managed in the workplace, so that employees know where they stand personally and when representing your business. And this is not a new phenomenon - our forerunners in business had to handle the introduction of the telephone, the social media platform of its day.

There is a story, possibly apocryphal, of a leading industrialist in the early part of the last century whose verdict on the telephone was published in the New York Times: "*Under no circumstances will we allow this in the workplace!*" The concept of employees communicating casually in a business setting, potentially making or breaking contracts accidentally on the *telephone*, was unthinkable.

These days, formal written communications are for specialists, and the familiar telephone plays second fiddle to email and social media platforms, but the same concerns should be raised: there are legal, cultural and management implications to every communication that originates within your business or team.

Getting your Social Media right

From the moment a new person states proudly on Facebook "I work HERE" they are representing your business. If this catches you unawares, then it's time to get online. Either set up a page which represents you properly and professionally and to which your employees can link themselves, or if you are in a security setting, for instance, make it very clear from the outset that there should be no crossover from personal to business activity.

This applies to all social media platforms - making sure that personal and business Twitter accounts are not confused, being careful about pinning on Pinterest or sharing on YouTube, and exercising a degree of care on LinkedIn.

Whatever your attitude to social media - and this will depend on its strategic importance to your business - you should have a clearly stated policy, formally laid out and included in your company handbook. If you depend on social media communication for promotion, customer service and communication you are likely to have a fairly open policy, so as you grow staying in control is essential.

Protecting your online presence

Hacking stories are all over the news, every week. Lost user details, stolen passwords, compromised bank accounts.... Online security isn't just a buzzword - it's something we all need to take seriously.

What does online security mean to you?
The first thing that should come to mind is getting good anti-virus software onto your PC or laptop. This is an absolute essential and must be kept up to date. And it doesn't need to cost anything: for personal use, most antivirus offerings have a basic free level. Businesses up to 10 employees can often benefit from free versions, too – check the small print! You don't want to be caught out using unlicensed software, do you?

Even if you think that your website doesn't merit attacks, there are people out there who would disagree. My own site security programme records thousands of 'botnet' automated attacks every year.

There's a similar risk out there in the world of social media - Twitter in particular is notorious for 'spam' links being generated in a way that is likely to attract your attention, and clicking on a link can expose your Twitter account or, more seriously, your PC, to abuse.

And what about the proliferation of phishing emails? We receive a handful most days, and they are getting cleverer in their language and their targeting. Some of the most alarming have included messages apparently generated by HM Revenue and Customs at the financial year end asking people to accept a tax refund, and an email we received apparently from Companies House asking us to re-confirm the submission of our Annual Return, only days after entering it. In the latter case, anti-virus software caught the message, but if this had slipped through them only the knowledge that a successful submission email had already been received would have prevented disaster.

Risk perception varies enormously. From Polar Bears to Penguins, along the whole SE/CE continuum, responses to this type of threat will be different and need to be managed accordingly. Make sure that everyone in your business – including you - is trained to recognise the risks that their life experiences do not cover.

Penguins: Aware of the danger, but can still be caught out.

There is a healthy amount of scepticism protecting Penguins
 from obvious phishing attempts - but a danger that limited exposure to things like social media will result in innocently following a link sent from a friend's hacked email or Twitter account. As fake emails become cleverer and more complex, it can be hard to keep up.

Think about setting up additional security on sites that you use. If you have the chance to set additional questions of the first school / favourite film / first pet variety, do this. Some sites can set up a code to be entered (sent to your mobile) if you try to sign into the account from a new browser. This prevents hacking directly into the account, but can be annoying to circumvent if you find yourself needing to log on from the back of beyond after having your phone stolen (I speak from experience!).

Ensuring that a good anti-virus screen is operating on your PC or laptop will remove a lot of the risk, as simply viewing an email will no longer result in a virus being transmitted. Avoid following links sent on emails or social media messages unless there is a detailed and credible context. Most viral links on Twitter are preceded by phishing phrases such as 'Look what this site says about you!' or 'I couldn't believe this!' Don't fall.... And if you are asked to click a link in an email to anything relating to money, don't: go into your account through your browser. Might be genuine, might not.

Remember, Penguins can also be too cautious and miss out on genuine email alerts and messages. Learning to screen what is dodgy and what is not is a skill that comes only with experience.

Polar Bears: Susceptible to temptation, without understanding the risks.

 Polar Bears can be too trusting, thinking they know how to handle the internet and are above the dangers it presents. The main risk is falling for phishing attacks offering rewards that look too good to be true.

There are documented cases of young staff members with access to commercially sensitive data revealing this inadvertently in an unsolicited 'quiz to win an iPad' or similar. For a business, this is the more risky end of the spectrum - losing some face online can be dealt with, but compromising business confidentiality and data protection is the greater threat.

Perfect Password Practice

Every site you sign up to, every email account, every online system – and some internal ones too – will ask you for a password. How do you keep on top of generating and remembering a multitude of random word strings?
There are a few handy techniques that will help to keep you safe online.

First, it is not a sin to write down your passwords and keep them in a safe place. The likelihood of a hacker being able to access a sheet of paper in a file in your office is extremely remote. You may also be improving the data security of your business if you keep a record: if anything happened to you, could others access all the information required to keep the business running? Most systems do have password resets, but there will always be something that is lost.

If you are going to keep a record of passwords and you want to be ultra-secure, then you can use a <u>random password generator</u>. Search online for one of the many sites which offer this, and record carefully and use what is generated. Here's one: WGUrmNnta7 - I would definitely write that down!

For passwords you are going to use day to day and need to remember, there are a number of techniques for building a secure string of characters.

Site specific strings
This is a good way to have different passwords for each site without causing total confusion. Make up a unique string of six or more characters which you can always remember.

It is not a sin to use parts of familiar names or dates in your passwords. If anything, this will improve your data security because you can remember this element easily. Don't use a whole name or a whole date, though – that's not secure. Instead, use the first few letters, or a jumble of initials.

Always include at least one 'special' character, and try to remember which one you have used. They could be $, %, {, * - use the one you like. Occasionally a site will require only letters and numbers in a password so you can simply leave out the special character for those sites. If you can't remember whether a site accepts special characters, you always have at least three attempts at logging in.

Once you have this familiar string, add three or four letters to identify the site. For example, your string could be SPG727$ and the identifier for Facebook could be "face". Your password for Facebook is therefore SPG727$face – for Twitter, SPG727$twit, and so on.

Keyboard runs

Tactile people – and good typists – will retain a muscle memory for their passwords. This is helpful for passwords which are dictated to you – determined automatically by a system. You can also make up a string that is comfortable to key in. For instance, % is shift+5. If when typing your password you naturally light on the 5 key then shifting to the special character is natural, and secure.

Finding patterns in preset or random passwords

This can be fun! Rather than changing a preset, secure, random password, look for patterns. This helps with PIN numbers, too. Look for the pattern on a keypad – do the numbers flow from corner to corner; what shape do they make? Look for familiar initials, abbreviations, words in your preset passwords. I have a preset random password for one service I use in which I saw an item of underwear and a film character. Unforgettable: once I think of those, I can recall the whole password without effort.

When and how to change your passwords

Be ready to change your passwords if required. If a social media account is compromised – the most common problem – you will be asked to change your password immediately. Often, internal systems will require a change on a regular basis – 30, 60 or 90 days. When you build your password string, have something that can be changed within it, or get into the habit of adding an identifier to the end – 01, b2 etc. And don't forget, it is not a sin to record your password securely – and it can be safer if you do so.

Data security within your business

Paper filing is becoming a thing of the past, as documents are all computer generated and our awareness of the carbon footprint grows. We are keeping valuable information electronically within our businesses - convenient, but potentially open to attack or loss.

Your databases and servers hold client information, contract details, personnel files, designs and other intellectual property.

It's important to work within the Data Protection Act to keep tabs on personal details, of course, but think wider than this: what would be the impact on the business if all this data was lost or corrupted?

Data security does of course cover resistance to attack from external sources, but a business needs to be sure that everything can be recovered in the event of system failure. Make sure that you are backing up your systems – regularly! There is nothing more frustrating than trying to recover data from a corrupted hard disk because the last backup is weeks or even months out of date. When did you last bring that portable hard disk in to the office? Is your data really secure? Consider using secure cloud backups which are scheduled to run nightly, automatically, and which keep your data safe offsite – there are many IT companies who offer this service.

Simply using cloud storage for documents solves part of the data loss problem, but what about the security of cloud services? Where is the data held? If you are keeping personal data – and by that we mean anything that could identify an individual, so it's a broad definition – then you have to be careful. There has to be consent for data to be transferred outside the European Union: do you know where your cloud servers are based? Are they in America, or the Far East? You have to be sure that the information is secure.

Information security needs to play an increasingly important role in business today - greater sophistication, automation, availability and ease-of-use of hacking tools means that our business assets are more at risk than ever.

Understanding how and where your business is most vulnerable allows you to make better, more informed decisions about where to target your internal policies and technologies in order to reduce any risks and minimise disruption in the event of your systems becoming compromised.

Securing your website

A website is essential for all businesses, and customers expect to be able to email you too, so what happens if disaster strikes? When Superstorm Sandy hit America's east coast in 2012, the direct hit on New York caused online chaos as hosting servers were flooded or taken down by power failure.

We may not be in the path of many hurricanes here in the UK, but we've seen some businesses cleaning up their online presence after the economic equivalent: the demise of website companies. If your domain name has been supplied as part of a website build package, and for any reason the original owner is unable to renew the registration, then there is a real danger that your website and email addresses will be lost.

The best way to protect yourself is to understand who owns

your company's domain. Search now on any hosting website for your own domain name, and click on the 'WHOis' link provided. This will give you a short report which tells you the identity of the registrant, the registrar (which is your end hosting provider), and the expiry date for the domain name registration. The registrant is the only person who can renew the domain! If the report doesn't say what you expect, have a chat with your developer or host about transferring the registration to you and make sure your contact details are up to date. There is a small fee, but it's worth it!

But what can you do if this doesn't yield results? Sadly, some companies find themselves with hosting in their developer's name, but there's been a fall out and the site is offline. There is no way to force a change. In situations like this, the only option is to speak nicely to the developer and see if they will transfer the ownership. If this fails you should first contact the domain registrar listed in the whois search, and if that fails contact the authoritative body. Each type of domain has a different authority – for .co.uk domains, this is Nominet, and for .com/net domains, it's ICANN. This final port of call can be extremely helpful and get you and your website back on track.

The Ticking Browser Timebomb

New users will be entering the online space now with up to date browsers, enjoying the dazzling functionality of websites built using HTML5, modern Javascript, CSS3 – standard in design and development – and good security to keep them safe.

Experienced users – the old hands – will be happily upgrading to the newest software to keep abreast of all the opportunities the internet has to offer. But what about the people who took that tentative step two or three years ago? There are plenty of instances of users being frustrated and left behind with the speed of technological change – and exposed to dangers which browser security improvements are intended to fight.

For those users who are most comfortable with a PC or laptop to start their journey, there is often confusion between the concept of an operating system and a browser. When both are installed at purchase, supplied by the same software house, it's easy for the uninitiated to assume that they are a single unit. This is a powerful argument for bringing individuals straight onto tablets and other mobile devices – updates are automatic and streamlined.

Laying down a challenge to the Polar Bears

If you know someone who's recently made the leap online, ask them which browser they are using. You'll be surprised when, after some searching, they come back with the answer 'Windows'. The distinction between a browser and an operating system is lost on a lot of Penguins, especially when there is a smooth transition between the two and they are bundled together by the software provider.

This applies to individuals and sole traders as well as people working within large organisations where their computer equipment is supplied by a central department.

For people who started their journey in the last few years, the problem is acute. I'm referring mainly to Microsoft technology, as it is the entry level for most new users – Mac or mobile users tend to be more technically aware, and alert to changes.

Why is there a problem?

Let's dig deeper into the timeframes: Some versions of Windows XP were still being supplied to new users in 2010. Vista, its much-maligned successor, started its lifecycle in 2007; Windows 7 in 2009. Anyone making the investment in a PC would expect their capital investment to last them a while. However, any hardware sold with these operating systems will have come with Internet Explorer 7 pre-installed. Users do not realise that this has a much shorter shelf-life!

IE7 has been superseded 4 times since its launch in 2006. Security has been improved with each iteration, and it's vital for people who are operating online without much background experience to have the maximum protection available. Over the last few years, the techniques of website development have moved with the browsers, so that new sites with new functionality simply don't work on the older versions – anything below IE9 is unsupported by virtually all developers. If you think the browser it came with is the only option for your PC, it could be easy to get frustrated by this whole internet thing!

A small step to make a difference

Although less than 2% of the world's internet users are still on older browser versions, there is a skew towards late adopters and older users- the people we need to encourage to use the internet effectively.

Here's some true stories:

A friend describes an older relative's frustration with websites that 'look dreadful' or 'don't work'. The PC is only a few years old and expected to last – they want their money's worth! Unfortunately, the user is comfortable with one particular browser that won't allow an upgrade unless the operating system is upgraded too – but the PC is too old to accept the new operating system. Because of a lack of support and understanding, the user effectively withdrew from using the internet, not realising that moving to a new browser could restore the good experience. Harmony has now been restored.

A client of mine panicked when their email account no longer accepted attachments. They took their laptop to their IT support consultant who poked and prodded, tested the hard disk, upgraded virus software, and pronounced himself stumped. They set up a new email account, thinking the old one had been compromised. Still no luck. Thanks to a chance conversation with us two frustrating days later, they upgraded their browser and hey presto! All working again.

A large organisation with a policy of simultaneously upgrading all its browsers missed a user, leaving them wondering why a new website design looked so poor. After terrible feedback on a new design, and criticism that functionality was missing, it finally dawned on everyone that only one PC had these issues. A quick call to IT provoked an apology and an upgrade – and the client is content.

Keeping browsers up to date can transform the user experience, and transform the lives of the users as well. It's a small step to make a difference!

The Communication Revolution

Understanding your Digital Footprint

As soon as a business is created, it has a Digital Footprint.

Information from Companies House, HMRC, telephone service providers, trade registers and news articles is available online. Data companies bundle this up and sell it to online directories, which then create free listings. Google picks up this information, and creates a Google+ page. You're being found in local search results, with a map to your office. The Digital Footprint is now visible to all your clients!

Customers post reviews – good or bad – on directories or Google, but you can't respond because you don't know they are there. A new employee adds your company to her Facebook profile – and Facebook creates a new page for you. A client, sitting waiting in reception, plays with his smartphone and 'checks in' to your location on Facebook or Foursquare. They comment on the service they received.

Suddenly, you have an online presence that you do not control.

This is the Digital Footprint of your business – wherever you walk, you leave an imprint. Managing that imprint and making it work for you is one of the most important skills you can learn. By understanding and managing the Digital Footprint – incorporating it into the spider's web of information you have to establish for your business – you learn more about the makeup on the online space than you can imagine.

You have a personal footprint, too, which can be created without your knowledge on social media as friends mention you or tag you in photographs. This can link up with the footprint of the business very quickly and expose your personal details to business contacts. Do you really want to have these worlds collide? Sometimes yes, if you are vital to the brand – but normally no. Learn to keep business and personal tracks separate.

Try this experiment: Search for your business name online. Search for your own name, as well, and see if the two are becoming inadvertently confused. It's important that the brand you present online is consistent.

Look through the first few pages of results – you may be astonished at what is already out there if you have been established for a while. Or you may be equally surprised to find nothing at all for a new business you thought was well represented online. It all depends on how the internet has managed to join up all the references to you and your business. The more coherent the picture – the clearer the footprint you make in the sand – then the easier it will be for people to find your business online.

The Online Spider's Web

Forget the World Wide Web – you are caught in a Spider's Web as information proliferates online. So how do you control this and turn it to your advantage?

First, you need to understand what the internet is seeing. It's not a whole lot different to a business on the high street. This is advice for Polar Bears and Penguins alike: you need to understand it before you can take advantage of it.

When you first start out, your business is stranded in the online equivalent of an out-of-the-way industrial estate. It's there, possibly a rival to Harrods, with all its signage and stock - but no-one knows about it. So how do people get to know where it is? Here's a few ways:

- A sign on a busy street pointing to the business. The online equivalent is a directory entry, Google+ local page, or similar.
- A news article in a local publication. Think about writing a blog to tell people what you do.
- Word of mouth. This is the most powerful tool in the real world, and online it's replaced by social media.

These are the fundamental building blocks of a Digital Footprint. By making sure that your business is at the centre of a web of information, you stand more chance of people finding you.

The concept of a web is crucial, too: it's no use having every social media channel known to man and a website and directory entries which don't refer to each other. Make sure your social media links are on your website. Put your website address on your social media profiles and online directory entries. Ensure that the language you use to describe your business is consistent across all these channels, using a few key descriptions of what you do.

But what happens as the business grows and you move to new premises? You wouldn't do a midnight flit and expect your customers to find you again without help, would you. The same is true online. Make sure that you keep all those signs up to date. Tell people what you're doing, where you're going, and keep your Digital Footprint fresh.

Search Engine Optimisation

Managing your Digital Footprint and developing the online Spider's Web is the core of what is known as Search Engine Optimisation. This is such a broad and ever-changing topic that we cannot address all the ins and outs here – there's a reason why good search engine optimisation is carried out by professionals who devote their time to making it work.

At the time of writing, the leading search engine in Europe – Google – has released yet another change to the way it selects websites to return in search. Increasingly, the focus is on good content on your website and everywhere else that you can be found online.

You can put the first building blocks of optimisation in place yourself to ensure that you can be found online. Develop that Spider's Web of information; make certain that what you say is consistent on your website and your other peripheral channels (social media, blogs, directories. Make everything about you on the internet both reflect your brand and inform the user about what you do. Content is King: getting this right is half the battle.

Starting the process
Here's an exercise: write down what your business does, but limit that sentence to 160 characters. It's not as easy as you think! Work out exactly what you do, what people might be looking for when they want your goods or services. Be very specific - it's all very well saying you give great customer service – but what do you actually DO. Nail down the detail. Be concise.

Done that? Good. What you have really done is:

- Written the metadescription for the homepage of your website. This is the short two line summary which appears under your site title on search results.
- Written your Twitter business profile summary – and put together material to help your social media strategy.
- Identified the simple key words which describe what you do; you can now expand on these in the content of your website, and explain them in more detail.

- Defined the sectors and descriptives for online directory and Google + page information.

This can also help you to get your business and its goals clear in your mind. Getting ready to shine online can also help your business define itself in the real world.

Social Media: how to choose?

You're busy working to build your business, but you have to keep the online space up to date with what you are doing. Social Media is an essential tool as it's the online equivalent of word of mouth recommendations – but it's a notorious time hoover. How do you manage this new communication tool without losing sight of the real goal?

There are many more opportunities to communicate online than anyone thinks.

This is the Conversation Prism, an ever-evolving representation of the different social channels. Developed and maintained by Brian Solis and JESS3 at www.theconversationprism.com, and reproduced here with their permission (visit the website for the fabulous colour version!), the detail is an eye-opener for anyone who thinks that social media is a narrow field or one which is likely to 'blow over'.

Every segment details the different communication channels in use for business, enterprise, social sharing, content, music, video, reviews, research.... There are so many applications for online communication of all types – the range is staggering.

With the scope of the Conversation Prism in mind, it's important that you don't take everyone and anyone's advice when choosing your strategy! Social Media does work for everyone – but not every social media channel is the same. If I tell you to buy size 10 jeans, will you blindly do that without making sure they fit first? They may be perfect for me – but one size does not fit all. Here's a rough guide to the current popular social media channels for business.

Facebook

Ever popular with the average Polar Bear, this is a favourite because of the degree of personal interaction and the familiarity with the platform. However, it works well for businesses selling direct to consumers – B2C – and those establishing a community around their location. It does not work well for the majority of business-to-business enterprises (B2B) other than as a way for employees to interact, or for small service companies interacting with other sole traders. If you do decide to set up on Facebook, pay close attention to their Terms and Conditions, and make sure you set up a distinct business page – not a personal profile – and try to appoint at least two administrators. If you have a problem with your own personal Facebook account, you could lose access to your page.

Twitter

Not as frightening as it first appears, Twitter is an extraordinary business tool. It is local and international, a resource as well as a way to communicate your news, personal and anonymous, appropriate for any type of business. It helps you to be concise and clear about what you do and attract the right type of clients and contacts. It's also addictive and time consuming unless managed properly!

There's plenty of advice about 'tweet every day or it won't work' which frightens many businesses. What do you tweet about? Intensive, managed campaigns are part of a cohesive marketing strategy, but when you start out, tweet when you have something to say. That way, you will attract the people who follow you for who you are, and you won't burn out before you reap the benefits.

When you set up your Twitter account, make sure that it's sending you notifications when someone mentions you, follows you, or retweets you, so that you can then go online and follow up that interaction. This is the best of both worlds: spend time in your business, but chat with the people who are spreading the word about your business when it suits you to do so.

YouTube

This is the world's second largest search engine, according to many statistics. If you do anything which has a visual aspect, You Tube is the internet equivalent of putting on a demonstration in a local shopping mall to attract people to your business.

Selling a car accessory? Record a video of how to fit it. People searching for your accessory may do so on YouTube, and the video will in any case appear in search on Google and other 'standard search engines. Never underestimate the power of video: it's getting more important every day.

LinkedIn

The home of business-to-business (B2B) companies: even if you are only small, a well-written LinkedIn listing for your company is

important. The site is so well established that often, when you start out, the first search result that will appear for you or your company is actually your personal or corporate profile page on LinkedIn. Another thread in the spider's web, it should never be ignored.

Pinterest

Fun and visual, Pinterest can be your dynamic window to the

world. Not known as a corporate tool, but used by many B2C organisations of all sizes, it's a valuable tool if your business or product is visual, colourful, crafty, fun, or emotive.

Using Social Media Management Tools

There are some great Social Media management tools out there – dashboards which allow you to handle three or four different channels at one time, or schedule posts way in advance.

Our current favourites are Hootsuite and BufferApp for simple scheduling and good reporting of the activity that comes from your social media strategy. They are invaluable for maintaining a social media presence if you are away from the office, for scheduling posts where you really need to get maximum exposure (for an event or an offer, for example) – but don't get carried away too soon! You need to know what you are doing.

There's also the opportunity to post from one social media channel to another. Post something on Facebook and have it immediately disseminated to Twitter? How useful! Well...... not really. If you don't use the different social media channels independently to begin with, you won't understand the nuances and differences between them.

You are talking to different audiences, and there is no shortcut here. Think about how you communicate with different people. Do you use the same technical jargon with customers and industry specialists? Do you chat about cake and coffee with your bank manager? So, would you post a serious message on LinkedIn and expect it to work for your consumer audience on Twitter? Would you post a short, snappy tweet and expect Facebook users to understand the Twitter shorthand?

Learn the ropes: then use the tools the way they are intended.

A learning opportunity

Social media isn't all about telling your story. There's a wealth of information out there to help you build your business and your understanding of the new world and your place in the market.

If you are a cautious Penguin who's not too sure about how to use a resource like Twitter, start by taking from it. Follow industry specialists – and competitors. Discoveries, papers, journals, blogs and news items are all posted as a matter of course on social media, and often across every channel (Twitter, YouTube, LinkedIn etc).

Impetuous Polar Bears can also learn from the world around them. Business practice, latest developments, changes to the legal framework will all be covered in online updates. Look out for things that you are not confident about, and use the online space to educate and inform.

Delivering Great Customer Service

Customer service has been turned on its head by the online space. Business no longer dictates, but is expected to listen – and customers expect an answer. With online media, dealing with customers seems to have been made simple, where in fact it's never been more complex!

Small businesses have to do it all, and getting the balance right is one of the biggest challenges SMEs can face. Developing your product or service, building awareness, networking or establishing a physical presence, delivering the goods, making sure the numbers add up, managing a growing business, supervising staff......

Customer service just adds to the pile, and it's often something which is neglected (because you've already made the sale, right?) or takes up too much valuable time (because you care) for no return. But get it right, and customer service excellence will build that bottom line.

Be Creative about Customer Contact

Make sure your customers believe they can contact you easily any time. There's nothing more frustrating as a consumer to find that the only way to ask a question is to make a phone call (premium rate?) between 9 and 5. Yes, it's unrealistic to expect an answer at all hours from a small business, but being able to post via a social media profile which is obviously active, or send an email easily, brings you and the customer closer together and avoids any frustration which could exacerbate a problem.

Use review sites appropriately

A new attraction I visited recently is fighting to be found in an area with a vast amount of established competition. As well as all the necessary things like a good website, well managed social media, and plenty of real world advertising and networking, they have invested in a well written Trip Advisor listing. They are carefully replying to all the comments, when they have time.

This simple interaction immediately sets them apart from other similar sites in a crowded market. Don't just sit and hope reviews work for you - show that you care about your customers.

Delegate social media!

There's a real fear of delegating social media accounts for the first time. But you wouldn't rush to deal alone with every telephone call, every email, every client walking through the door, would you? Social media is just another communication channel. Develop your own understanding of the strategy your business needs, set the rules and boundaries, and then let staff deal with the outside world while you concentrate on running your business.

Virtual office support

Many small business owners - particularly sole traders - find it impossible to 'switch off', getting trapped in the 'because I care' loop of being available to customers 24/7. Smartphones have a lot to answer for here, which is why my family confiscate mine at holiday time. However, customer service IS important and there are plenty of professionals out there who will babysit your social media accounts, emails and phone messages so you can get on with work or play without disruption.

Polar Bear or Penguin, these tools are for you!

 Ease of communication is the great reward of doing business online. By managing your client base effectively, you not only keep you customers happy but you give them a reason to spread the word about your services through the online space. By managing your staff effectively – whether Penguin or Polar Bear - you empower them to promote your business and their part in it.

Building Digital Skills

Key Skills for People and Businesses

    Polar Bears: You can change the world

    Penguins: Find your reason to dive in

DIY Disasters

Responsibility and Authority for Online Strategies

    Why can't the IT department handle your online strategy?

    Why can't the interns run your social media?

Implementing New Processes in your Organisation

    Climbing Everest: The Training Challenge

    "Seek first to understand"

What can you do today to help build Digital Skills?

Key Skills for People and Businesses

Polar Bears: You can change the world

Polar Bears in any walk of life have the chance to play a valuable role in helping individuals to build their Digital Skills. By recognising that there are people out there who aren't as internet savvy, adapting the accessibility of their services, and investing time and effort in helping others to develop their skills, Polar Bears can help to change the world.

Penguins: Find your reason to dive in

Can you think of one thing you hate doing that you would like to make more efficient, more effective, and generally faster and easier? It could be a personal task - or something in business which you really need to change to move forward.
If you have a goal in mind, something to aim for, the digital world stops being quite so daunting. It's just another, better way to do what you already do. And on the way to reaching that goal, you will develop your essential online skills – communicating, searching, informing and transacting.

DIY Disasters

There's a common myth that getting your business connected is child's play. If you are already using social media, then it must be simple to make a Facebook page, surely? And there are plenty of offers of free websites to get you started. Certainly, many small businesses take their first steps online alone, because the people running them are already socially engaged and think it is just an extension of their personal communication. But this approach certainly won't work for everyone – and doesn't work well for most people who try it. We spend a lot of time tidying up DIY efforts – just like in the real world when the ambitious plans to build your own extension go horribly askew.

It's true that there is a lot of free information out there to help you to get connected, and that's often attractive to new start-ups with limited funds. But there's also plenty of information on the internet telling me how to change the oil in my car. I can watch a plethora of videos on YouTube. I can join the forum for my make and model of car so I can ask other amateurs for help if I have problems. I can also find the best type of heavy duty cleaning products to tidy up the mess! You know what? I'd rather pay someone who does this sort of thing every day to do it properly.

Don't avoid paying for a service because you think you can do it yourself. Find the right professional to deliver the service to you. We all have cameras, but would you try to take the photos at your daughter's wedding? We can all cook, but how do you feel about knocking up a three-course gourmet meal to entertain your clients? I'm sure you'd give the same advice to anyone trying to DIY your area of expertise, too. So before jumping in with both feet, talk to an online business professional to get the job done properly.

Responsibility and Authority for Online Strategies

Sometimes it's the largest organisations that have the biggest challenge in embracing the online space. Despite having a huge range of skills across the whole spectrum of technical knowledge, there's a danger that online strategy can be sidelined.

Why can't the IT department handle your online strategy?

Your IT department are experts in their field. They know the ins and outs of networking, software, data security – but why should their expertise extend to the online space? They are specialists in a particular business support role. Do chemical companies expect their research scientists to publish marketing brochures along with patents? Can a construction engineer sell office space in the building they've built? So can you really expect a digital sector wizard, someone who manages the hardware you need to work effectively, or who is writing in multiple languages – PHP, C#, JavaScript, Ruby and hundreds more – or marking up the html and css background of the websites you visit every day, to be automatically skilled in the interactions of social media, the optimisation of content, the management of a customer base? Every business needs additional specialist skills to develop and grow, regardless of sector.

Why can't the interns run your social media?

This is a dilemma for business, but easily solved. It's likely that the young Polar Bears in your organisation are already fluent in the communication channels you want to use for your customers. They know how to work the tools – so let them! But as with any tool, their use still has to be supervised. Knowing how to work something is essential – but knowing what to do with it has to be taught. A child can kick a football around skilfully, but it takes training for them to play the game by the rules.

One of the biggest errors that large companies have made over the years is to hand social media to 'the intern' as if it is a closed box, something that the company should be seen to be doing, but not the preserve of senior management. Social media is part and parcel of a wider marketing strategy, and needs buy-in and direction from the top. In larger businesses the social media training normally starts with one person in the marketing department – it has to start somewhere – and the actual activity will be carried out by the most capable staff member at the time, but the key to success is the board looking carefully at what is being done, and staff carefully cascading knowledge and delegating responsibility where appropriate.

It's essential that the responsibility and authority for social media is cascaded from the top of the organisation. The biggest frustrations occur when a junior member of staff feels that they are battling against indifference and resistance from the top – from Penguins who have not sought to understand the potential or the workings of the online space.

Social Media is not a short-term commercial tool, but is key in building and strengthening the customer relationship, and to gain invaluable real-time feedback from the consumers that have kept the organisation in business for its entire history.

Implementing New Processes in your Organisation

Laying down procedures to secure the business and its data is the easy part – now you have to get everyone on board, and manage the policies you've spent time writing. Pushing someone to take on a new process when they are either sceptical or reluctant is a no-win situation. There are plenty of stories of staff running two systems in parallel because they don't trust the new one, or finding ways to circumvent new procedures to carry on as before.

Climbing Everest: The Training Challenge

Why would you climb Everest? George Mallory's answer was **'because it's there'**. Personally, before investing my time and effort in that sort of expedition I'd like to establish what I think is a good reason to go!

However, as a socially engaged individual, basking in Equatorial Warmth, I will happily play with anything technical online **'because it's there'** and I want to know all about it. But suggest this to the Penguins I know, older and/or less socially engaged colleagues, and the question is "**Why? What's in it for me?**"

There's a clear continuum of social engagement which ranges from suspicion to excitement – and it's a tough call to convince both ends of the spectrum to take the same things on board.

"Seek first to understand"

 There is a lot of scepticism among Penguins. Where interacting on computers did not come naturally from birth, the thought of taking processes and actions into a less familiar environment can be anathema. You have to give them a great reason to be there - which may not in fact be YOUR reason for being there.

Dr Stephen Covey defined the Seven Habits of Highly Successful People. Habit #5: To put your point across, to 'sell' the activity you want your staff to undertake, you have first to understand their point of view, and then couch your offering in their terms.

In any group, there is a likely to be a gulf of understanding between the least socially engaged and the fast learners. Simply going through a slideshow presentation or handing out a document won't cut it here. Instead, use the resources at your fingertips.

Let the Polar Bears come up with applications and ideas of how and where they will use new procedures, and how it applies to them. The half of the group that goes quiet will be learning from the discussion, identifying common ground, and discovering their own personal reason to take new skills on board.

If you can introduce your new thinking and policies so successfully that the Polar Bears are excited about a new toy, and the Penguins own a real reason to engage - now that's effective!

What can you do today to help build Digital Skills?

Polar Bears: be ready to make a difference

 You have the world at your feet, and by understanding the fiddly technical and legal risks you have made the journey towards the warmer climes and rich rewards of online business. But you also have a responsibility to help bring others in from the cold. Learn to disseminate your digital skills – and start with the browser challenge!

We are seeing more and more instances of people who have started their online journey being frustrated and left behind with the speed of technological change. You'll often find that someone's frustration with doing simple tasks online stems from the browser they are using! As the speed of change quickens, new websites simply don't work properly on older browsers, and it's something people just don't think of. So, ask the question, and help with downloading new. Keeping browsers up to date can transform the user experience, and transform the lives of the users as well.

Laying down a challenge to Penguins

Let's find the best reason in the world to get connected, and open up a whole new world.

Decide what is the most annoying, repetitive,

or frightening task of your day. With the exception of making coffee for the office, which as far as we can tell despite intensive research is still a manual exercise, it's a fair bet that a little time invested online will transform the task in hand. So, what's your bugbear? Here's a few we have tackled in the past.

- Working through and filing business cards from an event? – Find an app on your smartphone that will scan and catalogue them for you.
- Want to capitalise on those cards but shy on the phone? - Start interacting on Twitter and LinkedIn to consolidate contacts and build a relationship.
- Got something to tell the world, but used to doing it in print with long lead times? Look at blogging, online publishing, email newsletters to tell your story to a wider audience.
- Doing the books for your small business, but always on the move? – Take advantage of the growth in cloud-based accounting systems.
- Struggling to manage high volumes of paper files about your customers? – Find a virtual assistant who will transfer them to an online Customer Record Management (CRM) system.

Once you have your reason, you can build your skills. Once you have the skills, you can build your business online.

It's Time to Shine Online!

Are you ready for the challenges of the Digital Age?

Have you identified exactly where you started on the SE/CE curve? Were you a Penguin or a Polar Bear? So where are you now? Is it getting a little warmer out there?

Have you defined what you do in simple, concise terms and disseminated that information across all the right online channels?

Are you confident enough about how search and marketing work online to avoid wasting time and money on off-the-shelf internet solutions which don't suit your business? Can you resist the hollow promises of online success, free websites, or first page Google rankings which seem too good to be true?

Do you use the internet effectively to communicate with your customers? Have you picked the right channels to get the best results? Are you dealing with feedback and learning from the interactions?

Are you missing out on a market which isn't so internet-savvy? Can you anything to help them get connected, which will in turn increase your market?

Is everyone in your company or organisation happy with the strategies and processes you've put in place? Have you helped everyone find their reason to be online and support the development and progression of the business?

Do you know the risks as well as the rewards of doing business online? Have you ticked all the legal boxes, and made sure your data is secure?

Have you trained your staff to be aware of privacy, confidentiality, and the line between business and personal life? Do all of your employee handbooks and terms and conditions match up with your actions and expectations?

Do you get a slice of the £18.8 billion that's out there for the taking?

Grab that opportunity with both hands!

About the Author

Kate Baucherel BA(Hons) FCMA first worked in the digital sector for an IBM business partner in the USA in 1988, and was instantly hooked.

As a Chartered Management Accountant and company director she has in-depth experience of running businesses in industries from online media to manufacturing, construction, utilities, HR, sports and hospitality.

Kate understands that the day to day demands on businesses and on the people who run them can be overwhelming, and often prevent them from taking the simple steps that are needed to get to grips with new ways of communicating, networking, and attracting new clients and contacts. Kate helps enterprises to make the most of the online space without distracting from the real work, building small changes into established routines to make a world of difference.

A mum of two primary school children, Kate knows first hand the balancing act which goes with family and business life. The flexibility that is afforded by the internet is an invaluable tool for every facet of her life.

Acknowledgements

I'm incredibly grateful to all who have supported the creation of this book, particularly my very patient husband Xavier and our family, and my colleagues at Galia Digital and JDrew Creations. My thanks to Helen Turley, Matthew Kirk, Gillian Lewis and James Lane who read various parts of the work and offered suggestions and feedback, and to James Drew, Jordan McCord and Martin Ker for technical stuff and pictures.

More information about Go On UK, the drive to make the UK the most Digitally Skilled nation, and what you can do to find or offer help can be found at www.go-on.co.uk.

The internet use figures quoted throughout are from the Go ON UK /Booz and Company report which can be found on the Go ON UK website, and from the Office of National Statistics quarterly report into internet use for June 2013 and the three prior years.

The Facebook vs US Census age profile graph was first published on www.digitaltrends.com in April 2013 based on the Wolfram Alpha analysis of Facebook data.

The Conversation Prism is reproduced with permission of Brian Solis. Visit www.theconversationprism.com to see the full colour version in all its glory.

Also from MX Publishing

Simon Horton

"Horton gives practical advice on how you can get the best deal from any situation either in the office or in your spare time. Book of the Month."

Director Magazine, Institute of Directors

Also from MX Publishing

This book isn't for the faint hearted, the 73 rules to influence the interview have taken the best from psychology, NLP and uncovered the secrets that master influencers, successful pick-up artists, powerful business leaders and notorious con artists use to get whatever they desire. We have taken the best of what these manipulators can offer and made it relevant to the job interview, increasing your chances of securing the job you want. Chris Delaney a Careers Advisor and Hypnotherapist, reveals how to succeed in these competitive times, breaking down how to influence the interview into 73 rules. A mixture of stories, anecdotes, step by step techniques and psychology experiments explained, makes this book a fascinating read. While reading this guide you will see that the text embeds most of the 73 rules into your subconscious with minimum effort, to teach you how to influence the job interview.

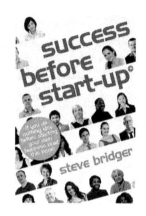

Success before Start-Up shares the start-up experiences of 19 small businesses; giving invaluable practical advice on the right business to match your abilities, on marketing, finance and planning. It is written by people who started just like you; who want you to succeed, and give you respect for wanting the same.

STRESS FREE
IN THREE
MINUTES

BY THE ENGLISH SISTERS

You may be feeling stressed right now or would like to help someone that is feeling stressed. It has been proven that heart attacks, strokes, high blood pressure, headaches, ulcers and many more medical conditions can all be brought on or made worse by cumulative stress. Stress has negative effects in all spheres of your life and can be fatal. The English Sisters, known as the Everyday Hypnotherapists, will take you on a relaxing journey in each of their easy-to-read short stories, which guide you into a comfortable stress-free state of mind in only three minutes.

Lightning Source UK Ltd.
Milton Keynes UK
UKOW06f1630231017
311512UK00006B/695/P